FACES

ROGER HUTCHISON

FACES

A Love Story

PARACLETE PRESS
BREWSTER, MASSACHUSETTS

2021 First Printing

Faces: A Love Story

ISBN 978-1-64060-637-1

The Paraclete Press name and logo (dove on cross) are trademarks of Paraclete Press, Inc.

Library of Congress Cataloging-in-Publication Data

Names: Hutchison, Roger, author.
Title: Faces : a love story / Roger Hutchison.
Description: Brewster, Massachusetts : Paraclete Press, 2021. | Summary: "A beautifully illustrated reminder that God paints his love on every face he creates"-- Provided by publisher.
Identifiers: LCCN 2020032027 | ISBN 9781640606371 | ISBN 9781640606388 (epub) | ISBN 9781640606395 (pdf)
Subjects: LCSH: God (Christianity)--Miscellanea. | Theological anthropology--Christianity--Miscellanea.
Classification: LCC BT103 .H88 2021 | DDC 231.7--dc23
LC record available at https://lccn.loc.gov/2020032027

10 9 8 7 6 5 4 3 2 1

Published by Paraclete Press
Brewster, Massachusetts
www.paracletepress.com

Manufactured by PRINPIA Co., Ltd.
54, Gasanro 9-Gil, Geumcheon-gu, Seoul 08513, Korea
Printed in September 2020, Seoul, South Korea

For

Atticus, Amelia, and Tennyson

I see your dad's face in yours.

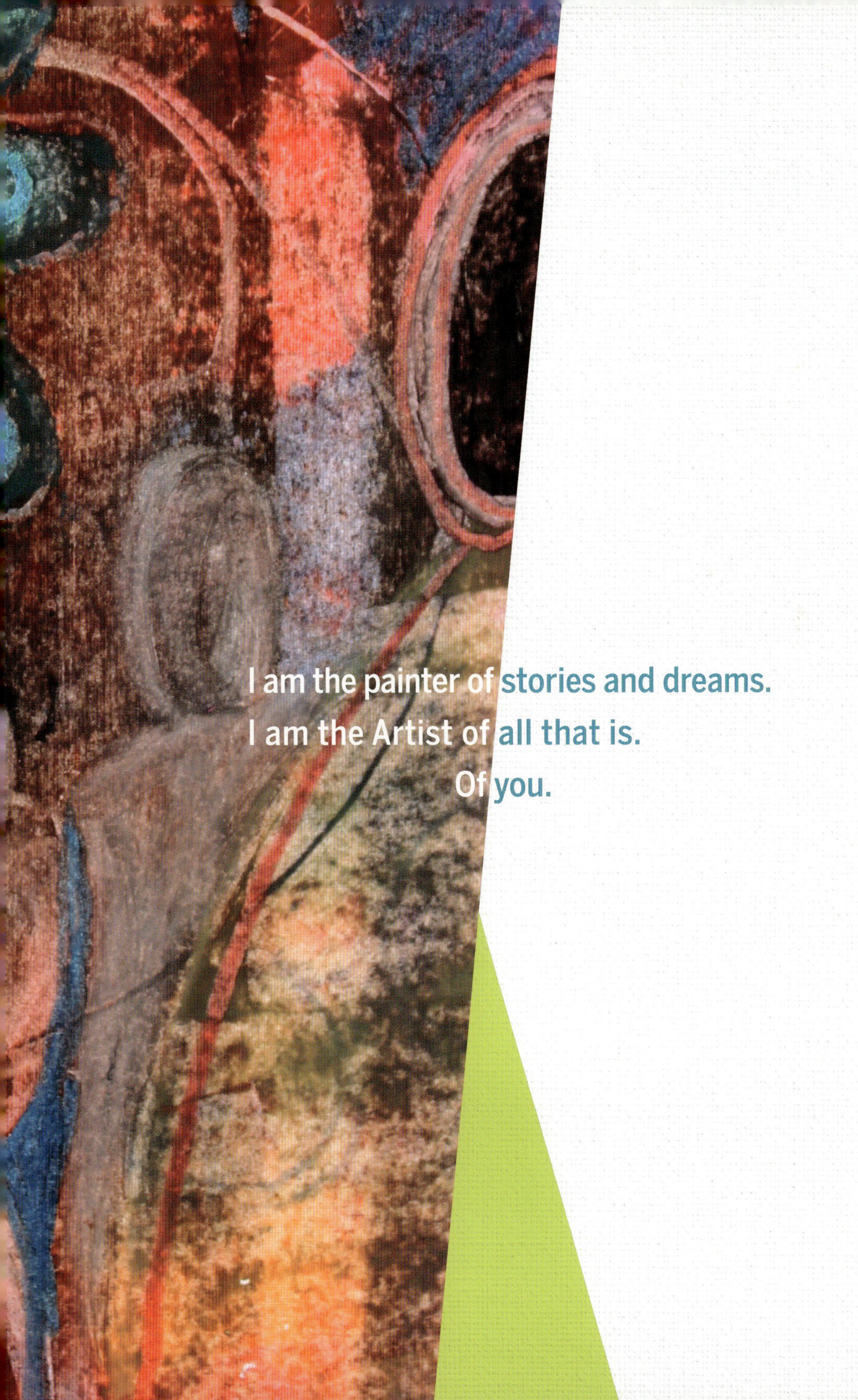

I am the painter of stories and dreams.
I am the Artist of all that is.
Of you.

I paint

mahogany lips and
warm honey skin

turquoise iris and
chestnut hair

umber freckles and
espresso brows
alabaster smile and
olive dimples.

My palette is filled with the colors of water and sky

colors of Me
colors of you
colors of Us.

I gaze at your face from a distance,
but also, from very close.
Know that I long to be close
to you.

We are separated by all of our assumptions,
preconceptions,
misunderstandings,
even a pandemic of fear.
So much mistrust.

Yet . . .

I know there is a longing in your hearts and souls

to touch

to know

to walk with each other.

We brush against each other.
Our laughter fills the space around us—
held aloft by a warm spring breeze.

I am the Artist Who has painted all our faces.

Every face that you see.

Faces you see on the street.
Faces of those you look up to.
Faces that perhaps you have turned away from,
for any number of reasons.

Faces that you remember from the past.
Every face that shows Me in one way or another.
Faces that you may be afraid of because you have forgotten ***how to trust.***

We forget.
It is time to face our fears.

You can tell the age of a tree
by the number of rings on her trunk
but only if you cut her down.

Her branches

stretched and expansive

gnarled and scarred.

A parable told in bark—

wise and strong.

Beneath her shade, there's *refuge.*

Deep wrinkles frame the tree's smile.

In the same way, bespectacled eyes sparkle and shine.

Every sacred life

is stretched and expansive

gnarled and scarred

by *love* and *loss*.

Still, we smile,

wise, weary, and strong.

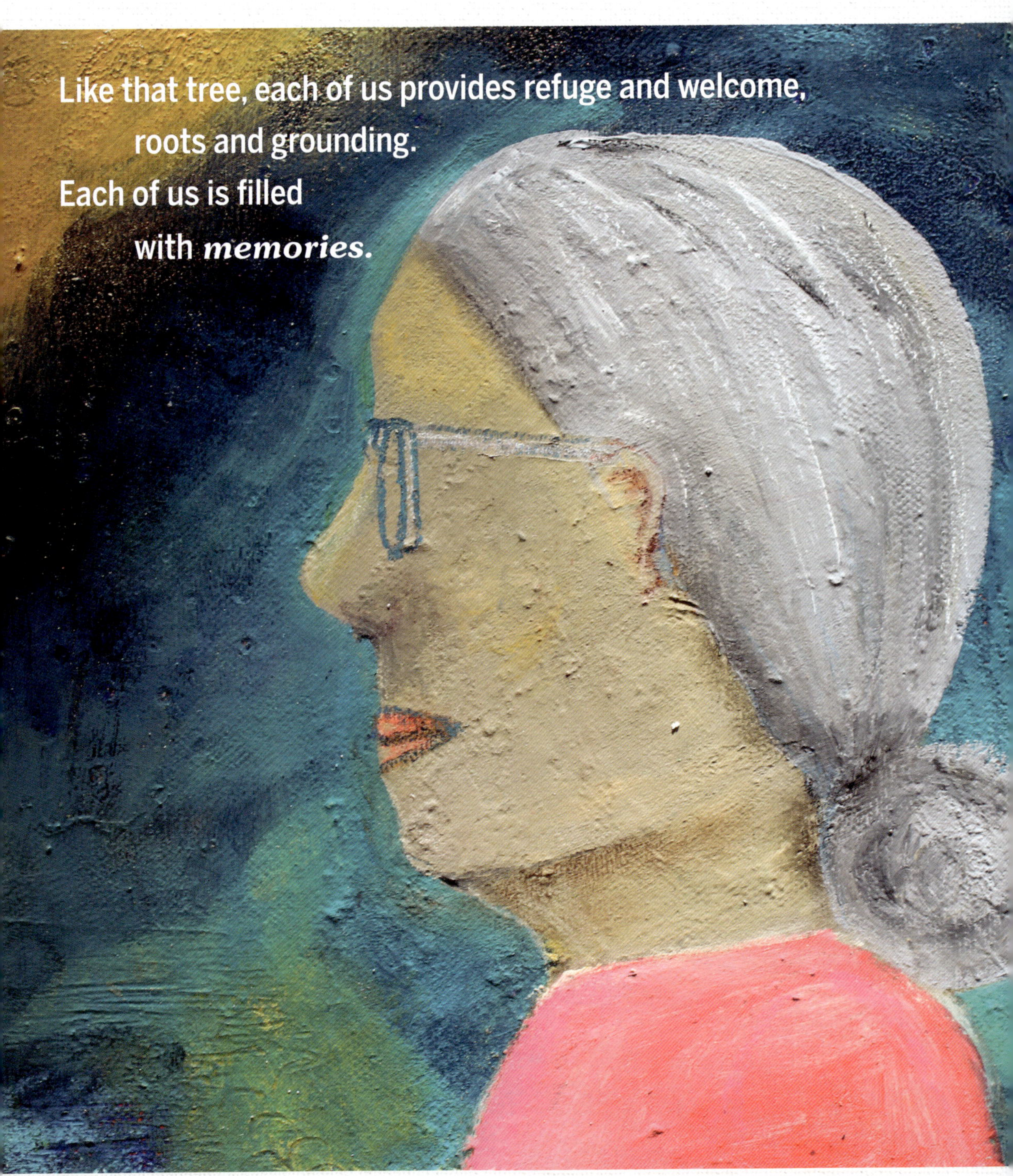

Like that tree, each of us provides refuge and welcome,
roots and grounding.
Each of us is filled
with ***memories.***

A bird cannot fly without
wings.
A sailboat cannot sail without
wind.
A life cannot thrive without
kindness
from others,
from ourselves.

There are such boundless differences
and beauty in every face I have made.

Can you even see how beautiful you are?

Can you fathom how much I love you—

your ***Creator***

the ***I AM***

the ***Alpha***

the ***Omega***?

When devotion pours forth
from the chalice
of your soul—
I am there and I smile.

I created you—

each of you, a masterpiece.

Your vibrant colors swirl and spin across the canvas.

I take your hand

and we dance.

My breath – ***your breath.***

My heart – ***your heart.***

There is no greater love than
Our Love.

When you are afraid,

call My name.

When you are alone,

reach for Me.

When you are filled with thanksgiving,

tell Me.

I will never leave you.

I am always here.

I created you and I love you.

Nothing will ever separate us.

I weep with you when you are sad. I celebrate with you when you are filled with joy.

I listen when you rage. I hold you close when exhaustion overwhelms.

And when the time comes, and you breathe your last breath,

I will welcome you home.

My beautiful child. My precious one.

Do not be afraid. Do not be afraid.

I am the painter of stories and dreams.
I am the Artist of all that is. Of you.

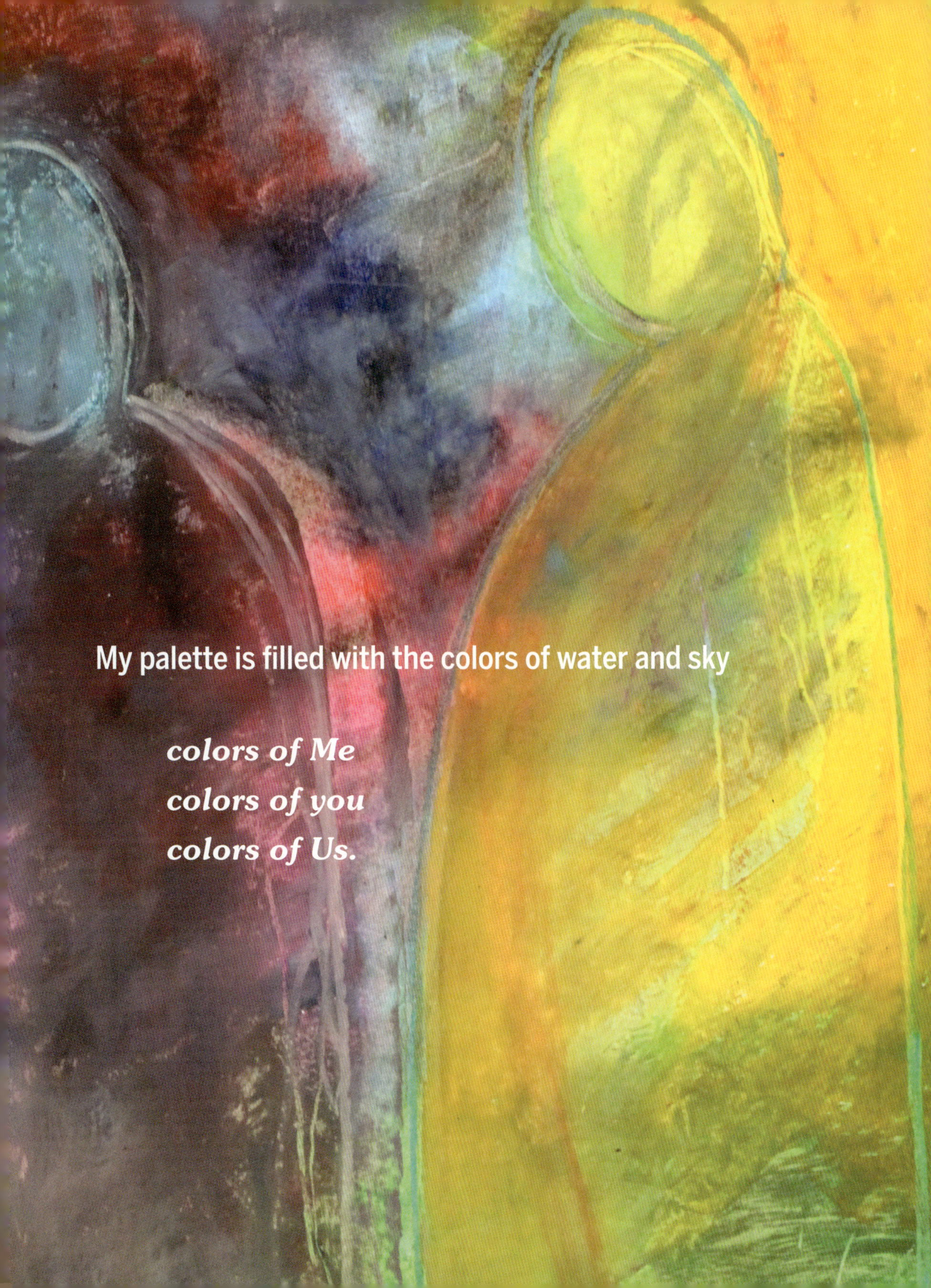

My palette is filled with the colors of water and sky

colors of Me
colors of you
colors of Us.